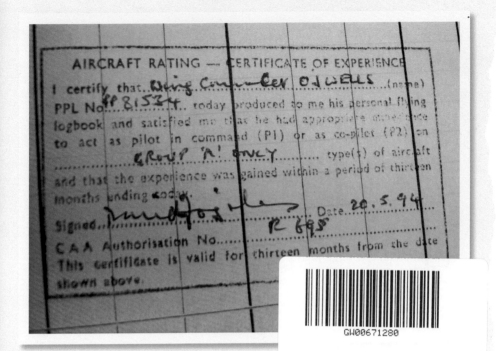

PREFACE

OLIVER WELLS WAS BORN on 10th March 1922 into the Charles Wells brewing family, the youngest of nine children, three of whom were to lose their lives in combat in World War Two. His affinity with aviation may have been inspired by his great-uncle Jack Capper, one of the founders of British military aviation. His elder brother James was Commanding Officer of 600 (City of London) Squadron RAuxAF and had lost his life leading a ground attack operation over Holland on May 10th 1940. Oliver clearly had a natural aptitude for all manner of flying tasks.

Following ab initio training on Tiger Moths in July and August 1941 and advanced training on twin engined Airspeed Oxfords at Cranwell from August to October 1941 and being rated as an above average pilot on both courses, Oliver was posted to an E.F.T.S. at Cambridge to become a flying instructor. The main task was to take pupil pilots up to first solo stage, following which they were sent abroad for further training if considered suitable. Quite a responsible job for a 19 year old. During 1942 he also took part in a rather odd experiment, the story of which follows...

CHAPTER ONE

EXPERIMENTAL NIGHT FLYING TRAINING 1942

BY OLIVER WELLS

IT MAY COME AS A SURPRISE to the average modern pilot to hear that some 68 years ago six unsuspecting would-be pilots were chosen for the honour of being trained to fly by night only, from the very beginning. I was involved on the fringe of this as a 19 year old ab initio instructor at No. 22 E.F.T.S. Cambridge, and the reasons for this rather odd experiment are not entirely clear, but it may well have had something to do with the need for speeding up the supply and quality of night-fighter pilots. Sir Arthur Marshall, formerly chairman of Marshall's Aviation, was closely involved with the details of the experiment and has kindly given me some useful facts which prompt my memory of those far off days of 1942.

It does not take a great effort of imagination to visualise the difficulties of teaching a pupil who had never flown before how to take off and land a Tiger Moth, control the aircraft and navigate entirely in the dark, and some detail of how this was successfully accomplished is worth recording. In order to evaluate two different techniques, the six cadets were divided into two batches, three being trained to fly by visual indications and feel, with the instruments as a secondary side, and the other three by instruments using visual indications as a very secondary side. The three instructors, headed by Wing Commander A.D. Bennett, the Unit C.O., had one cadet from each batch, and in the event both methods proved possible, but the visual cadets were delayed by the need to wait for suitable conditions when some reference to the ground was available. It was decided that introduction to day flying would take place after each cadet had flown solo at night.

Four Tiger Moths were fitted with artificial horizons in each cockpit and a single electric flare path was used with an approach path indicator and two gooseneck flares as rendezvous lights. Both Cambridge Airfield and the relief landing ground at Caxton Gibbet, at the intersection of the A45 St. Neots to Cambridge road and the Old North Road, were used. The aircraft were also equipped with a wing tip flare for emergency use if a forced landing became necessary, a device which certainly added to the general

Tiger Moth instructor's cockpit

excitement of such an occasion. Later the aircraft were fitted with a full blind flying panel, the directional gyro being a much more useful aid than the turn and bank indicator for keeping straight on take-off and climb and a twin flare path was also introduced.

The cadets were given ground instruction on the aircraft equipment, cockpit drill and propeller swinging, lectures on night flying procedure, including lights used on the airfields, effects of controls and reading of instruments, and the three instrument cadets were given Link Trainer experience. They were also told how lucky they were to be the pioneers of such an interesting trial and asked to raise difficulties or suggestions on the training and keep notes of their reactions.

Early in January 1942, a far from ideal time of year when the cadets were likely to be numb with cold in the back cockpit of the Tiger Moth when they weren't paralysed with fright, the flying started with the instrument cadets being given experience of the feel of the controls and instrument reactions to their use, which is of course rather different from the Link Trainer. The visual cadets were given experience of the effect of the controls, straight and level climbing, gliding, stalling and medium turns.

A modified patter was adopted by the instructors to suit the night conditions. Reference was made to stars and land marked beacons and sometimes a faintly visible horizon or bank of clouds allied with reference to the artificial horizon. Recovery from a spin could not be taught owing to the unsuitability of the Moth battery fittings for such a manoeuvre apart from any other considerations, so emphasis was placed on familiarity with the stall and recovery, both with and without the engine, and the attitude and feel of this manoeuvre. There was a tendency for cadets to be unconcerned by unusual flying attitudes or speeds since darkness cloaked the fact that the ground was in the wrong place or rushing up to meet them, but they were firmly taught to avoid steep turns or violent manoeuvres. Obviously, navigation in blackout England was a difficult problem, not that cross-country flights were contemplated in this trial, and reliance had to be placed on airfield beacons and rendezvous lights. There was usually some light leakage from Cambridge railway station in those days of steam trains. This general familiarisation stage took an average of just over three hours of dual instruction before the circuit procedures were introduced. Take-off was started well to the right of the flare path so that the line of flares could be seen from the rear cockpit, and a fairly tail down attitude adopted (control column thumb against the compass corrector box) to avoid possible propeller damage and naturally the hand of the instructor was acting as a long stop in the early stages. Keeping straight along the line of flares was soon mastered, but there was a tendency on the climb to wander off to the right when making the intended straight ahead climb to 800 feet due partly to the lag in the turn indicator until the full effect of the venturi was reached.

This sometimes resulted in the flare path being lost underneath the aircraft after the turn down wind. Following the straight ahead climb a continuous turn of just under rate 1 on to the down-wind leg was made. This had to be visual since the cadets had not enough experience to complete the turn on the magnetic compass without chasing the needle all over the sky.

Initially a cross-wind approach to finals was tried, but at this angle the approach path indicator, which of course gave a white light for too much altitude, green for the correct approach path and red if too low, was not visible, and cadets had difficulty in judging their rate of descent when coming across wind, ending up too high or too low the final turn into wind. It was found better to fly down-wind until well past No. 1 flare, so that the line of flares could be seen over the left shoulder; when a medium turn of 180° would position the aircraft for a longish straight approach into wind, with time to adjust the rate of descent to keep in the green sector of the approach path indicator. This also eliminated turns near the ground by very inexperienced cadets. There was a tendency to approach wide of the flares, more than 50 yards out, making it more difficult to keep straight and judge height. This had to be corrected; between 25 and 50 yards being about right. Having successfully kept in the green of the approach path indicator, cadets were taught to level off when close to No. 1 flare and usually keep on a little engine until the aircraft sank onto its wheels; then allowing the tail to sink under its own weight moving the control column back only slightly. Cadets were encouraged to use the throttle intelligently if the landing was not working out according to plan. During this circuit training little difference in ability was found between the instrument and the visual trained cadets. In some cases attempts to see the ground and judge landing height by the light of the downward identity lights were made, and this had to be discouraged since the angle of the flare path gave a much more reliable guide. All six cadets completed their first solo flights at night, having never flown in daylight, after an average of 16 1/2 hours dual instruction – a very creditable effort. Curiously, there were some advantages over day first solos; the take-off and landing runs were fixed and the wind direction could virtually be ignored, the flare path having been laid down into wind. The approach path indicator gave a very accurate rate of descent, clearly indicating under or over shooting and, perhaps most important, there were no risks of collision. In daylight we often operated up to 30 aircraft in the circuit at Cambridge and such incidents were by no means unknown. After some 25 hours dual and 6 solo the cadets were introduced to day flying for the first time, having been given lectures on aerodrome rules and safety measures, particularly the need to keep a good look out. Recovery from spins was the first priority, and each cadet soloed

in just over an hour, using wheel landings as taught for night use. The art of navigation was naturally lacking in the early stages and extra instruction needed to be given. Aerobatics were then mastered after an initial disinclination to execute violent manoeuvres which stemmed from the night instruction.

It can be imagined that this trial was not without its traumas for the instructors. On one occasion I took off at night with a pupil for circuit training at Caxton Gibbet, only to see a bank of East Anglian fog just about to blot out the flare path. Following a very tight circuit and landing I was just in time to see the tail light of a solo pupil climbing off the flare path. Fortunately he kept his head and eventually force-landed at Oakington after an anxious half hour for all concerned. Thanks to the magnificent reliability of the Gipsy Major engine the wing tip flare never had to be used in anger for a forced landing as the chances of a successful arrival were remote.

It was concluded and proved that it was possible to teach a pilot to fly safely by night using only instruments or external visual references, but that for accuracy and safety in all conditions the ability to fly by instruments was essential. Although wheel landings were taught and used safely at night, the provision of tricycle undercarriages would have saved time and reduced the risk of accidents. All six cadets were recommended for night fighter training and must have been justly proud of their most unusual introduction to the skies.

CHAPTER TWO

PATHFINDER DUTIES 1943

"An account of my experiences from September '43 to February '44" - Flt./Lieut. O.J. WELLS, R.A.F.

(After training Oliver joined 7 Squadron based at Oakington in July 1943. 7 Squadron had been the first to equip with the Short Stirling 4-engined bomber back in late 1940 and now formed part of the recently created Pathfinder force, with a mix of Stirlings and Lancasters, which the squadron had started to take on charge in May of that year. Oliver's first trips were flown on Stirlings, including one mission when he and his crew bombed Hamburg in a thunderstorm – 'we couldn't work out the lightning from flak'. He then graduated to Lancasters, taking part in the raid on the Peenemunde V-2 rocket factory on August 17th. On the night of August 30th he took charge of JA710 MG-N a Lancaster B.III with only 80 airframe flying hours on the clock.....)

PART 1. The end of Lancaster "N" for Nuts

ON MONDAY, AUGUST 30TH it was announced that we were to bomb a war production factory at Munchen Gladbach, on the edge of the Rhur. This was the tenth night I had been out that month, as the weather had been very fine for operating. The Take-off was late, about 00.30 hours, as the moon would not be down until the early hours of the morning. At the briefing, we were detailed to go in late in the raid, actually 26 minutes after zero hour, to back up the target markers. Formerly we had always attacked around zero hour, and I think we all felt prejudiced against this change. I pointed out that the defences would be less effective, and was pleased with the idea of being over the target at the end of a raid to see how the fires would be going. It was the shortest raid we had been briefed for, being only four hours from take-off to landing, and should have been the easiest.

We took off soon after midnight, and set course. Here a word about the crew. I had the greatest confidence in all of them. Fred, the navigator, quick witted and efficient, had proved his efficiency and ability to keep us from straying, and deal with the unforeseen difficulties which always crop up from time to time. Johnny, the bomb-aimer, another officer member of the crew, was very much on the ball, not only at his own job, but able to cope efficiently with most of the aircraft's equipment. At dropping bombs he had shown what he could do on the Peenemunde raid, where he got a photograph proving a direct hit on the target factory. Bob, the engineer, had the engines and fuel system buttoned up, and I never had much worry about petrol shortage or mishandled engines. Steve, the wireless-operator, a sleepy Newfoundlander, did his job quite satisfactorily with a bit of chasing. Al, the Mid-upper Gunner, had not been

with us long, seemed quiet and steady, and immensely keen. Tom, the Rear Gunner, provided us with some wizard cockney humour from down that end, and was an excellent gunner. As a crew I think we worked very happily together, and I would not have changed any of them for the pick of Bomber Command. I don't think we were over-confident, since we had a long attack by a Ju 88 on our first operation, and so knew that they existed all right. On this occasion the gunners came out very well. Provided that a fighter was seen before it attacked, we felt we could cope all right, and with the flak you just took your chance.

This Monday night everything went well until we were approaching the target, and were able to see the attack going well ahead of us. It was a fine night, pleasantly dark with no moon and a cloudless sky. The rear gunner reported a combat in progress on our port side, and I made my stock remark about not watching it, but watching for the rest of the sky. Very soon after this there was a series of sickening flashes, yellow streaks, and metallic clangs. This was just to the left of my pilot's seat, and I realized that the port wing had caught a packet. Simultaneously the rear gunner called up to report the attack, asking me to turn like hell to port. It was just a second or two too late, but the gunners cannot see everything all the time, and there was always that chance of getting jumped.

Then Tom called up again to tell me that it was a Me 110 that had attacked us. The answer he got was that I didn't care a b—what it was, but watch like hell in case it comes back. Immediately after the wing had been hit, a fire had started. I dived the aircraft, to try to blow out the flames, but this was useless. Then I feathered the port inner engine, and used the fire-extinguisher. I didn't expect this to do much good, as the fire seemed to be behind the fireproof bulkhead of the engine, and it didn't.

It was then certain that the main petrol tank had caught it. The fire was getting somewhat out of hand by now, with the flames stretching back from the trailing edge of the wing to beyond the tail. It was making a noise above that of the engines, like a giant blow-lamp. I felt as a sort of flying beacon we would be meat for even the dimmest night-fighter pilot. I had kept up a pretty violent jinking all the time, to make a second attack more difficult. It didn't take long to decide that it was all up, and I told Johnny to jettison the bombs. When he reported that this was done, I gave the order to abandon aircraft. In doing this I felt a curious sense of unreality, as we had so often practised it on the ground, and it was hard to realise that this time they were doing it in earnest.

It must be understood that although this takes some time to describe, the actual time from being hit to my order to abandon aircraft was little more than two minutes.

Johnny was first in the order to go out, and of course the front escape hatch stuck fast. This hatch is in the floor of the nose. He has told me since that he had to break it open with an axe. To me, at the controls, the delay seemed an age, though it was probably not more than one minute. Then Johnny went, followed by Bob, Fred, and Steve. The last fixed my 'chute on me whilst waiting in the queue.

It was very strange and empty in the cockpit when they had gone, with the wind whistling in through the open hatch. I decide to wait for a bit, as I knew that the mid-upper gunner would take some time to get clear of his turret, and out of the door, which would be difficult to open. I hoped he was being quick, as the kite was getting in a very bad way.

Then suddenly there was some sort of explosion. The nose of the aircraft dropped, and she started to spiral down to port in a sort of skidding spin. The controls were useless, and I decided it was high time I wasn't there. The altimeter was dropping down from 12,000 feet when I last looked at it. I left the seat, and lurched towards the front escape hatch. Having reached this all right, I made a dive out of it. My head and shoulders cleared it all right, but there was a tremendous sideways force of air, which blew me against the side of the hatch, and I stuck fast. No amount of struggling and kicking would get me free, and I could see some lights on the ground, seemingly above me, going round and round, and coming towards me. I was shouting and cursing, but also thinking quite clearly for me. I saw the position was hopeless, and that I would be killed, and wondered what it would be like. All the time I was physically occupied in trying to get free. The last thing I can remember doing was releasing my parachute harness, to see if I could shake it free, and bail out hanging on to it. I thought I must be caught up by that.

Here there is a blank, for reasons unknown. My next impression was

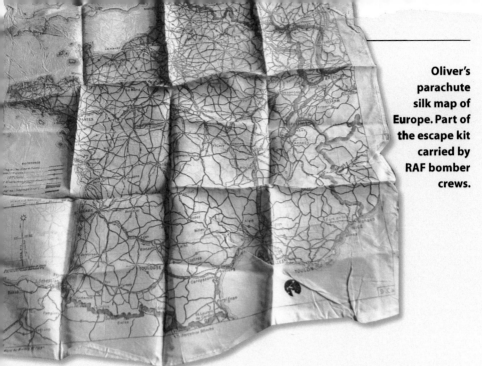

Oliver's parachute silk map of Europe. Part of the escape kit carried by RAF bomber crews.

wondering what I was doing face downwards on the grass. I lay there for a moment thinking how good and firm it felt. Then I remembered the spin, and that according to myself I was supposed to be dead. Lifting my head soon put me wise: over to my right was the remains of the aircraft, somewhat spread about, and a mass of flames and white hot metal. The remains of the fuselage was burning from end to end, but curiously the right way up. Since I had been in the escape hatch at the bottom of this, I can only assume it did a few revolutions on hitting the ground.

I wondered what sort of shape I was in. My face felt a bit queer, and I couldn't focus my right eye. Putting my hand up revealed a good deal of blood on the right side. Then I stood up, finding to my great relief that my legs were intact. I couldn't lift my right arm,

and it seemed rather painful. I thought at first it was broken, but after gingerly investigating decided it was only the collar-bone, as that seemed the centre of the pain.

My Mae-West life jacket was still on, but no parachute or harness, and the loose suede flying boots I had been wearing were no longer on my feet.

Looking round, the country seemed to be an open heath, with small bushes. To the east I could see the target blazing over the horizon; it was then that I heard a motor-bike coming, and decided it was time to make myself scarce.

I heard later that the crew all got out safely, and were duly captured after a varying period of a few days. The rear gunner has since told me that the turret and tail blew right off in that explosion, so it isn't surprising that the poor old Lanc went out of control.

PART 2. Exit from Germany...

FEELING INSIDE MY battledress, I found the packet of concentrated escape food and wallet containing a map and money. Then I set off, keeping to the edges of the fields and small farm paths. I decided to try to put a good distance between myself and what remained of the kite before dawn. The going was a bit rough, and I realised that until my feet hardened a bit, the going would be slow. The chief snag was treading on unseen stones in the dark.

As soon as the sky began to lighten in the east, I looked round for a hiding place. It wasn't long before I came to a large thicket, surrounded by rushes in some marshy ground. Here the cover seemed quite good, and I settled down for some sleep. The Mae-West made a good pillow.

I woke up about nine o'clock, (fortunately my watch was still going) to find that my face had stopped bleeding. The shoulder was stiff, and the pain more dull. The thicket seemed to be a good hiding place, and my only fear was that my track through the rushes would be seen, I knew, however, that the Germans would find the remains of my 'chute in the kite, as they don't burn right up when tightly packed, and would probably write me off as killed in the aircraft. Also the fact that I didn't have any boots or shoes made my footprints almost negligible.

Looking over my equipment, I studied the small handkerchief map. It was obvious that with its lack of detail it would only be useful for approximate bearings. The money wallet, much to my disgust, contained only French francs, designed for an operation over France. I should have had one containing German, Dutch, and Belgian money too. I cursed the man responsible, whom I pictured sitting smugly in the Mess back home.

On this first day I experienced a sort of futile rage against providence, that it had to be my crew that caught it. Once all reasonable precautions have been taken, it becomes largely a matter of luck, and ours hadn't held. It was obvious that this fury wouldn't do any good. I would have to make the best of it, and concentrate on getting back.

I didn't feel like eating that day, so decided to keep the food till I really needed it. For water I knew I must wait until it was dark again. The day passed slowly, and as soon as it was dark again, I prepared to move on. My aim was to keep west, and get into Belgium or France, and there try to find help in the underground organization.

After I had been going a short time, I came to a fairly large river. A search of the bank revealed no sign of a bridge or boat, so I decided that enough time had been wasted, and I would have to swim across. Having got my clothes off, I tied them in a bundle with the escape food and packet of maps.

Then I slipped into the water, holding the bundle on my head with my good arm, and kicked my way across. The noise seemed colossal, and I expected half the neighbourhood to meet me on the far bank. Arriving there, everything was still quiet, and I lay down for a bit to rest. I had drunk all the water I wanted, and my clothes were still dry. Starting to dress, I found to my horror that the packet of food was missing. This must have fallen out of the bundle into the water, and I cursed myself for my carelessness. There was also a sock missing, but this I replaced by putting the French beret, which I always carried, round my foot, and tying it on with my scarf. Then I set off again, still fuming about the food packet.

Keeping mainly on the field paths, and using the stars as a guide, which I found more handy than a compass, I padded on west until day began again. This time I found a haystack, and covering myself completely, soon fell asleep. When I woke up in the late morning, I found a farmer and his wife working in the field about fifty yards from the haystack. They stayed there all day, and I dared not stir at all, in case they heard the hay rustle. Eventually it was dark again, and I was glad to leave the place. The country was quite easy going; flat field paths, and small villages. I found that after midnight it was quite safe to pass through the villages. Occasionally a dog would bark behind a gate, and make me jump about a yard, but nobody seemed to take any notice of them. I was beginning to feel pretty hungry, but decided not to try a burglary, as it didn't seem worth the risk of getting caught.

Letter from 7 Squadron's Commanding Officer to Oliver's father.

When daylight came again, I found another haystack, rather more secluded. Later in the day, when I was awake, I heard footsteps, and male voices. They came right up to the stack where I was, and pulled away the hay. I thought it was all up, until one of them exclaimed in French. It turned out that they were French workers doing forced labour on this German farm. I told them what I was, and they looked extremely scared. I asked for food, but they said they had none, Then I asked where I was, and was told it was about fifteen kilometres west to Aix-la-Chapelle. They left me, and I spent ages looking for this town on the map, not knowing in my ignorance that it was Aachen. The next night I came to a big railway yard, which seemed to stretch for miles, and was illuminated by lamp posts. I tried to cross this, but getting half way across in a dark spot, found several workers ahead and so retreated. Whilst

I was wondering how to get across, my problem was solved by an air-raid alarm. All the lights went out, and everyone scattered. I walked serenely across the eight lines, and through the store houses without seeing anyone.

Soon after this I was searching an orchard, as I usually did when I passed one. This time I saw some round black shapes in a tree above me. Giving the tree a violent shake, which set the farm dog into a tirade of barking, I collected quite a lot of apples, and, at a safe distance, ate about four. They were very hard and sour, and I guessed that daylight would reveal a somewhat green exterior. This worried me not at all, and, being the first edible thing I had found in the Fatherland, tasted marvellous. The rest of them I kept in my battledress blouse. When it started to get light, I had for the first time a lot of difficulty in finding a hiding place. The country was very open, but at last I found a fir spinney and bedded down in some bushes. I put the apples on the ground, and went off to sleep. When I woke up at about eight o'clock, the daylight showed my position to be very public. I therefore quickly and sleepily decamped, and found some better undergrowth. Waking again later, I found that in my drowsiness and panic, I had forgotten the apples, and simply could not find them. This made me wild for the rest of the day.

The following night was quite uneventful, and I made quite good progress. At one point I tried to milk a cow, but couldn't seem to get much joy out of it. The wretched thing got rather hot and bothered, and started making a lot of noise, so I gave it up.

I found a very secluded wood to lie up in the next day. During the day I tried to make some pads for my feet out of the Mae-West, as they were getting very sore from treading on things in the dark. This wasn't a success, as they wouldn't stay on. In the local village near the wood they seemed to be having some sort of fete that day. They sang German military songs for hours on end, and I wished them all in hell.

The next night I skirted a town, and passed through some concrete pillars, which seemed to be a sort of feeble tank trap. Later in the night I saw a red light in the road ahead of me, and wondered if it could be the frontier. I decided to lie up in a convenient haystack, and see if it was still there the next day. During the day some children came and played hide-and-seek round the hay-stack I was in. I thought they were sure to bounce onto the step of hay where I was, and wondered if I would try to tie them up or paralyse them with fright whilst I got away. However, in the end they went off, and the rest of the day was peaceful. When it was dark, I returned to the road and found the red light was still there. Then I went back into the fields and went carefully on parallel to the road. There was an extra thick wire fence, but this was easily passed, and there were no more signs of a frontier. The next day I hid in a large wood, and, wandering round, found some scraps of newspaper written in Dutch. This was positive proof that I was now in Holland, and, best of all, I might get some food. As soon as it was getting dark, I went down to the nearest farm, and attracted the attention of an old woman there. I had been working myself up for this moment, and was depressed by the frightened and cold reception I was given. The whole household came out to look at me, and I made it abundantly clear that I was of the R.A.F. and very hungry.

After a consultation amongst themselves, they made signs which I eventually took to mean that I was to be taken to a house where they spoke English. A small boy then led me down a track to a single line railway. Here there was a crossing, and a small house. I went up to the house, announced by a yapping dog. A middle aged man came out and realised at once what I was. He gave me a most profuse welcome, and led me into the house. Here I met his wife and 21 year old son, who had learnt a bit of English at school. I explained my plight to the latter, and soon found some ham and eggs before me, followed by bread and jam and tea. This was Monday night, and the last meal I had had was in the Mess on the Monday evening before, prior to take-off, and so I did full justice to the meal. In fact I foolishly ate rather a lot, and suffered for it later. They offered me a bed for the night, which I gladly accepted. It was great to settle down in bed, instead of trekking through the dark.

Next morning I borrowed a razor and shaved. The first look in the mirror rather startled me. There was a scar all down the right side of my face

(fortunately not deep), and the white of my right eye was completely red. A week's stubble completed the picture of a very ugly customer.

During the day I was concealed in an out-house across the railway line, and enjoyed a good rest. They had a radio hidden in there and that day I heard the news of the invasion of Italy. The father came along with two pairs of old shoes that he had procured. They were both much too small, but I gratefully took the larger of the two pairs.

That night I decided to go on. The mother was obviously terribly nervous all the time, and they evidently had no connections with any underground movement. Their son gave me his rain-coat, probably his only coat, and the mother a scarf. I felt bad about taking these things, and being able to offer nothing in return, but the coat covered my battle dress, and meant I could walk in daylight, and so was very useful. A map showed me I was in the southern tip of Holland, and only a few miles from the Belgian frontier. I decided to make my way through Belgium into France, trying to contact the underground movement, which I will call "The Organization" from now on.

I left an R.A.F. button as a souvenir for the son, and the father put me on the right road for the Belgium frontier. I made better progress with some food inside me, and the shoes on, although they were horribly tight.

Early next morning I crossed the railway line, which seemed to form part of the frontier. There were no guards in evidence, and the crossing seemed simple enough. I heard many stories later from the Belgians about shootings at the frontier, and so concluded that luck was on my side just then.

During the day it seemed all right to keep going by keeping to the woods and fields. In my raincoat I didn't seem to attract more attention from the peasants than a curious glance. When it was dark, I tried a farmhouse by the road. Here they spoke French, of course, so I was able to converse to a certain extent, and at least understand them all right. They gave me some food and milk, but were very frightened, so I left directly afterwards. The nearest large town was Liege, and they directed me towards it. After sleeping a bit during the night, I pressed on towards Liege.

In the morning I saw the town ahead of me, and decided to skirt around the side of it, carrying on west. During the day I passed a lot of people including a party of German soldiers. Fortunately there were quite a lot of ragged specimens about, and I didn't excite much comment.

By the evening I had by-passed the town, and found myself walking along the river towards a large village. Owing to the under-sized shoes, my feet were badly blistered, and extremely sore. I therefore decided to try and get some help in the village.

After crossing a bridge over the river, I climbed up through the village on the west side.

Having no luck over contacting the organization in small farms, it seemed to me better to try a larger and more prosperous looking house in the hope that they would have more contacts. There were some villas standing in their own gardens at the end of the village, and I selected the last one. After a careful survey, to make sure I wasn't seen going in, (this was important, because the locals were apt to gossip about an unusual looking visitor) I entered the garden and went up to the door.

Right: **Oliver on the run working his way through the Belgian Underground. This picture was taken in broad daylight in his Belgian hosts' back garden.**

Part 3.
Belgian Hospitality and the 'Organization'

JUST OUTSIDE THE DOOR I found a very chic middle-aged lady, whom I startled almost out of her wits by the following blunt address in school-boy French, "Madame, I am an English airman, and I want food and help."

She rallied round very quickly, and took me into the hall. Then she called Gaston, a young fellow about my age, who spoke English of a sort.

He asked me some questions about my identity, and I showed him my wings, identity disc, maps, compass, and so forth. He was soon convinced that I was a genuine Englishman, and became most effusive, and presented me to the rest of the family. There was Madame Leduc, a charming old lady, and owner of the villa. Her daughter, Madame Schoonbroodt, whom I met first, M. Schoonbroodt, Jacqueline and Monica, their two daughters and lastly Gaston, who was engaged to Monica.

I was again the first airman to come their way, but it soon became very obvious that I had fallen on my feet in no mean fashion, and the relief and feeling of relaxation was marvellous. The best of it was that they didn't exhibit any panic, though fully aware of the danger, and assumed that I would stay there as a matter of course.

After a hot bath and a change of clothes, my feet were bathed and patched up by Jacqueline, and some comfortable slippers provided. Next came a large supper, followed by liquor brandy and a cigar. The contrast between this and the last ten days was so striking that I kept wondering if I was awake.

I was given a nice little bedroom with a deep feather bed, and slept like a log. On the next day Gaston told me that they knew an old lady who was in touch with the organization. Later that day I was introduce to Mlle. Delwaide, a Godly looking old lady, hung about with crucifixes and lace. She told me she could help me to get home. She took my name, rank, and service number, and promised to come back.

I told her my chief concerns were firstly to let my parents know that I was alive, and secondly to get back to England as quickly as possible. She said she thought I might get to Lisbon in ten days. In two days she came back with an elderly gentleman, who was running this section of the organization. They told me that they had contacted England over their secret transmitter, and had been told that I was all right. They always make this check, since members of the Gestapo sometimes tried to get into the organization to find out all about it. If they were found to be German agents they were quietly eliminated. Mlle. Delwaide told me that since they had contacted England about me, my parents would have been told that I was all right. This took a great load off my mind; I little knew that this message, and two subsequent ones were kept secret.

My parents heard nothing, and were even told by the Air Ministry in February to give up all hope of my being alive. This indicates that the cheering stories I was frequently told in the organization, of R.A.F. men caught with them, and shot out of hand by the Gestapo, were certainly true.

Mlle. Delwaide and her companion, (who was later murdered in a concentration camp) told me that there was a broken link in the route down to Spain, so that I would have to wait for sometime. The system was that an airman was passed from one guide to another all along the route. If one guide was caught or gave up the whole system was held up whilst an organiser went off to replace him.

I waited five weeks in Tilf, the village where the villa was. The days were long and I was very impatient to get going, but the route was still out of action. I wanted to go off on my own by bicycle, but they were all convinced that I stood no chance of getting away like that, and I was finally dissuaded.

The Schoonbroodts were very kind. I was made to feel quite at home, and fed all the time very well. Their food was almost entirely procured in the black market, as the official ration was negligible. When my feet had healed, they bought me a new pair of boots made to fit me. There were many other acts of consideration and kindness too numerous to mention.

After staying in this villa for five weeks, I was moved into Liege, from where the journey started. It was arranged that I was to go to the house of one of Mlle. Delwaide's friends. This was No. 45, Rue Monulphe, and Mlle. Fifi Fraipont lived there.

Here I must include the story of this family. In 1941, Fifi had started to help the R.A.F. One day she took an Air Gunner to her home, where her old father and English mother lived. One of the neighbours talked and the Gestapo arrived, arresting her parents and her married sister. Fifi herself was not there at the time. After six terrible months they were condemned to death. Fifi, who has some influential friends, got a petition signed by the Queen Mother of the Belgians, and the sentence was commuted to life imprisonment in Germany. Her sister was made to work in a saw factory in Rhur, where the workers were chained to the machines, even during air raids.

Fifi, undaunted, continued to work in the organization, feeling, I believe, that nothing mattered any more but beating the Germans.

When I was taken to stay in this house, where the arrests had been made, I thought it rather asking for trouble. It was explained, however, that if you work right under the noses of the Germans they usually failed to spot it. The house was still in a complete shambles. The Gestapo had searched it after the arrests, and turned everything upside down, Fifi was too upset to tackle the task of straightening it all out, and lived on her own in three rooms at the top of the house.

The day after I arrived there, I started a fever, and felt deadly. After a day in bed, Fifi, against my will, fetched a doctor. He was a small quiet man, who had attended several airmen. He didn't seem to know what the trouble was, but also had a look at my collar bone. This apparently had set itself, and although crooked was quite firm.

The next day revealed me a bright yellow, and it was obvious that the complaint was jaundice. I soon felt better, but was yellow for quite a time. I think it must have been caused by being without food for a time and then eating too much, After it was over I felt more fit than I had done since the prang. Fifi was kindness itself and completely spoilt me with delicacies out of the Black Market which she couldn't possibly afford.

Whilst I was ill, the route had reopened, and I missed a chance of leaving, which was very galling.

When I was fit again, I was taken to see a Catholic priest, who wished to help me. He had the sort of face one trusts immediately, and from the start I felt he was the most able man I had met over there.

He told me that far too many were being caught on the way to Spain, many being sold to the Germans. He therefore proposed to get in touch with a friend of his, who could get me picked up by air. This sounded an excellent scheme to me, and I accepted immediately. Fifi didn't like the train route either, as she had known several fellows who had been caught on it. The priest promised that I should go as soon as possible, but said it would take a week or two to organise it.

Waiting was very irksome, but Fifi did everything possible to make things easier. During the day it was necessary to keep in the house, and avoid being seen at the windows. After dark we often went out, either to visit friends, or occasionally to the cinema. The films at the latter were poor, but I found the German news-reels very interesting. The propaganda was undoubtedly clever. It was a curious sensation to sit next to a German in a cinema or tram and know that I only had to say a word or two to give him the shock of a lifetime. They all looked so smug and arrogant, and it was pleasant to be fooling them.

One day a friend came to the house very early, telling us that the Germans had blocked both ends of the street, and were searching the houses. I dressed hurriedly and got out of the house and down a side alley in double quick time. Later in the day we heard that they had called off the search, and I was able to go back.

Another day the police told Fifi they were eliminating a Belgian in the next house, who was collaborating with the Germans. This would have brought a veritable hornet's nest of Gestapo about our ears, and Fifi managed to stop the proposed shooting at the last moment.

On the whole things were quiet enough. Several times the main force of Bomber Command passed over the town, and I was able to appreciate the kick it gave to the people of the occupied countries.

Mlle. Delwaide brought me several lists of odd airmen staying in the town, in the hope some of my crew might be around. This was a very long shot though, and I got no results.

Fifi, although not a Catholic, used to go to the priest's church. Here she would go to the priest for Confession, and receive whispered instructions for me through the curtain. The greatest care was necessary because the priest was continually watched, and Fifi was of course well known because of the former trouble.

Unfortunately there was trouble with this route too, and the service was not functioning regularly. Fifi and I were always looking round for good escape routes. I felt that the usual ones were getting a bit worn, and it would be very useful to start a new one.

We got in touch with a railway official, and arranged that I could travel underneath the coal of an engine tender, in a sort of coffin. The snag was that the engine drivers after Paris were a very doubtful quantity, and it looked as if one might get stuck or turned in half way to Spain.

Then one day the priest's secretary came rushing round in floods of tears, to say that the priest had been arrested. She had managed to get to his office and destroy the papers about the organization just before the Gestapo arrived to search it. Although the arrest proved to be for helping some Jews it meant that that route was cut off for me. (I have heard recently, to my great sorrow, that this priest died in a concentration camp. He was a very fine man).

I had to get in touch with the first

organization, asking to be taken by train after all. I had possessed for some time an identity card as a student in Liege. This was the genuine article, provided by the police, with my photo, and the correct stamps. Armed with this and civilian clothes, I could pass as a student, provided that I didn't have to do much talking.

After another delay, I finally left Liege on December 20th for Brussels. At another house in Liege, known in the organization as a maison de passage, I was introduced to the guide, and another R.A.F. pilot. The guide was a young girl, apparently about fourteen, with a school-girl smock and hat. I was somewhat alarmed that this small object should be responsible for getting us to Brussels. The explanation was soon forthcoming. She was really twenty three years old, but had a young face. In this disguise as a school-girl, with straight hair, a fringe, and short white socks, there was less chance of her deadly dangerous occupation being spotted. She had in fact a large score of airmen successfully transported to her credit.

We went to the station and had a slow and uneventful journey to Brussels. I thought the other pilot with me seemed wrong somehow. When I could get him alone, I started asking him a few awkward questions. He then confided in me that he was not in the R.A.F. at all, but a secret service agent. He had been working in Germany and Holland, but his usual escape route had been cut off, and he was trying to get back through the organization of the R.A.F. That was his story anyhow, and he certainly spoke perfect English. His position was tricky since he couldn't give an R.A.F. number, and they told me he might be eliminated as a German agent. I heard later that he was cleared, and left Brussels, fortunately, just before I did.

Arriving in Brussels, I was taken to a small house, and photographed for some more identity papers. The ones I had on me had been used up, and some more were needed for the French papers.

Then I was taken to a small flat in the suburbs, where I was to stay until they were ready to take me on. This flat belonged to Susanne and Albert De Jonge. The former spoke English very well, and Albert was learning. They were both young, and Susanne had a brother in England. They were extremely kind, and made me most welcome. Their flat was very small, and I slept on a divan in the sitting-room. We had to be careful about noise. Theirs was the top flat, and the two flats below shared the stairs. They dared not risk letting the lower tenants know that I was there, so any time we came in together Albert would take off his shoes, so that they would only hear two people coming in or out. When Susanne and Albert were both out, I had to be very quiet. I was able to listen to the B.B.C., as indeed I had done all the time in Belgium, but unfortunately the radio broke down just before Christmas. Susanne dared not let her parents know what she was up to, so they had to go to her home for the celebrations in the normal way.

Copy of 'La Libre Belgique', the Belgian Resistance newspaper, complete with cutaway drawing of a Lancaster

I was taken to another house, where they were looking after an R.A.F. Wireless Operator from a Halifax squadron. We celebrated with wine and a mixture of ribald French and English jokes. He was a nice fellow, and I only hope he had better luck.

I stayed a fortnight in the flat there, waiting for the French papers to arrive. Eventually they were brought along. There was an identity card, a carte de travaile, and a special permission to enter coastal areas. There was also a new Belgian identity card, on which I was a commercial traveller for a firm of timber merchants. To these papers I gave some rough treatment so that they no longer appeared new.

The French papers were sewn into a secret pocket in the front of my trousers, to be kept out of the way until we had crossed the frontier.

I left on January 3rd and Susanne and Albert took me into the centre of town. Here we met the pseudo school-girl again, with a Sergeant pilot called John, who was to accompany me. I said good-bye to the De Jonges, and the girl took us along to the station. Here she introduced us to a young fellow, who was to be our guide. We boarded a very crowded train going to Paris. Our intention was to get off just before the frontier, cross it on foot at night, and continue on the train to Paris the next day.

Part 4.
Under the Gestapo

THE TRAIN LEFT VERY LATE, and for two hours everything went well. We were standing at the end of a corridor, the guide, John, and I. Then suddenly three men in plain clothes came up to the guide, and demanded to see his papers. There was something wrong with these, and they asked a lot of questions. Then they asked for John's papers and mine. I handed over my identity card, and they looked at this, then demanded my worker's permit. Unfortunately I had not been given one of these, since they didn't anticipate any trouble in reaching the frontier, and of course I had the complete French papers to use after we were across.

They took the three of us along to a carriage reserved for Germans and searched us.

Fortunately they didn't find the French papers, and I had nothing on me that disclosed my true identity. After asking a lot more questions they accused John and me of being British airmen. Both our accents were very pronounced, and we were caught out over our supposed occupations rather badly. Of course, we swore blind we were Belgians, and pretended not to understand English.

They commented, "You don't speak French properly, or German, and you say you don't speak English. What do you speak?"

One fat and persuasive Gestapo man said, "Haw, haw, you make me lorf", and proceeded to lose his temper rapidly.

Finally we both admitted we were escaping R.A.F. men, as it was so painfully obvious; it was clear that in any case they had no intention of releasing us.

We gave our correct names, ranks, and numbers, and were sent to sit with some German officers. These made themselves as pleasant as a German can, and asked a lot of questions about my aircraft and crash. They thought I was most unreasonable when I wouldn't even tell them what it was, or what I did in it. Although pleasant to John and myself, these officers gloated over the capture of the guide, pulling imaginary triggers at him, and telling him how he would be shot. This was hard to bear, but there was nothing for it at the time.

I managed to get to the lavatory and dispose of the French papers. We were taken across the Frontier into Lille, and here we were handcuffed together, and taken to the Gestapo H.Q., to the accompaniment of frightened and sympathetic glances from the French. After a short wait, during which time we were exhibit 'A', the journey continued to Loos, where there is a huge civilian prison.

Here after having all personal effects taken away we were separated. I was taken to a cell in which there were three Frenchmen and a Pole. The cell measured twelve feet by eight, and had a tiny barred window high in the wall. The floor and walls were stone, with very ancient and filthy straw pailasssses to sleep on, and one blanket. Being the last comer, I had to sleep with my head next to the sanitation bucket. This was no joke especially when it was in use. The routine was vegetable soup, (mostly grass) in the morning, with a little bread and ersatz coffee. The same sort of soup in the evening completed the day's meals. The soup always had a large earth and sand content at the bottom. All prisoners were given a sort of shower once a fortnight, and a shave every ten days. A five minutes walk round the courtyard every two days completed the routine. Cutting one's finger nails with an old bit of glass is not one of life's pleasures. One became quite adept at judging the time by the position of the sun on the wall, and, since no lights were allowed, we had to go to bed when it was dark, at about six.

My cell mates were all political prisoners. A gendarme, suspected of underground activities. A Polish café proprietor, who claimed not to know why he was there. A French rag-and-bone man, who was quite the most dirty and foul mouthed specimen I ever hope to live with, He had worms, of which he was inordinately proud, and talked of all day. Fortunately his Patois was so strong that I could hardly understand a word he said. He was there because he had hidden a man who claimed to be a Russian. When caught he proved to be a German deserter. Lastly there was a French shopman, who had helped some airmen to get through. He showed me a terrible scar on his back, inflicted by the Gestapo in an attempt to elicit information.

I was interrogated by the Gestapo about every three days. They wanted to know where I had been, and who had helped me. I kept this to myself, and threats soon took the place of persuasion. There was a lot of revolver flourishing, and talk of execution as a spy, but no physical violence. I gathered from the questions they asked that they had our "school-girl" under observation. Instead of arresting her they watched her and arrested some of the other guides when they could catch them with airmen. They had seen us board the train at Brussels.

Eventually, after several fruitless meetings, they said that at least I must give them the names of my crew, so that they could check my identity like that. This I refused to do, because I just refused to give any information on principle. However, I decided afterwards that after five months the crew must either be prisoners or home, so next time I had an interrogation, I gave them their names, not without some misgivings. I thought that when they discovered that I had been knocking around for four months there might be a terrible scene.

Much to my surprise, three days later I was called out of my cell and found John waiting to move. We left the prison after a stay of about a month, and I was never so glad to see the last of any place.

We travelled with some bewildered American airmen, who had been in England the day before, to the Luftwaffe interrogation centre at Frankfurt. Here, although in solitary confinement, I found it luxurious after the French prison. The interrogators decided that if the Gestapo had had a try, they wouldn't get much out of me, and after three days I left for the transit camp. Here my civilian clothes were taken away, and the Red Cross provided a uniform. This was a great relief. I had by then had quite enough of cracks about civilian clothes and spying.

It was good to see the recent prisoners, and hear the latest news from England. After a marvellous shower and change of clothes, a batch of us left for Stalag Luft 3.

At the transit camp I first saw and appreciated the really wonderful work done by the Red Cross, the food, clothing, and cigarettes provided there made life seem worth living again.

Oliver photographed by the Gestapo

Note
The Belgian guide who was with us was taken to Germany, and sentenced to death. The Third American Army arrived just before his execution, and he is now recovering in Belgium.

(The story up till now had been written after my repatriation in June 1945 following the end of the European war whilst it was still fresh in my mind and to satisfy the curiosity of friends and relations about my missing five months. The then current R.A.F slang reads rather oddly after over sixty years but it is better left untouched as a period piece. There had been some loose ends and my grandchildren wanted to know what happened next.

At the time I did not feel inclined to describe the rather frustrating and miserable life in prison camp, no place to be at the age of 21, and was more concerned with the future, but there are some incidents which should perhaps be recorded. One small incident on leaving the terrible prison at Loos in France that I had missed out was that to my great surprise my small valuables including a good watch and a signet ring which had been removed from me on arrival were handed back on departure.)

CHAPTER THREE

INCARCERATION, THE LONG MARCH AND REPATRIATION

ON ARRIVAL AT STALAG LUFT III near Sagan in Lower Silesia I was regarded with some suspicion by the senior R.A.F. inmates as I had been on the loose in Europe for several months and could have been a stool pigeon planted by the Germans. I had nobody to confirm my story of a rather unusual survival. Fortunately it did not take long to convince them on interrogation that I was a genuine R.A.F. officer. After that I settled down into the P.O.W. routine of taking turns with the chores (we lived twelve to a room), taking regular exercise, trying to plan an escape, reading and playing bridge in the evenings.

My initial card home through the Red Cross was the first news my parents had that I was safe (having already been notified that I must be presumed dead), and my mother's reply was a masterpiece of condensing the home news of five months into a small letter-card which was all that was allowed. It contained the news that, inter alia, my much loved childhood nurse, who had remained at home, had died of cancer, and that my father had been made a Baronet in the 1944 New Year's Honours List, something which at least partly must have reflected his family's war effort – eight out of nine children in uniform and three sons killed in action. Each prisoner was allowed one

parcel from home of limited weight through the Red Cross. My mother took expert advice and sent my R.A.F. greatcoat, a voluminous and warm garment made of good Melton cloth. At the time I thought it might have been more interesting, but had good cause to thank her foresight later on. Throughout this time we received fairly regular news from the B.B.C. on a secret radio obtained by bribing the German guards with Red Cross cigarettes or chocolate in exchange for the necessary parts. Once they had accepted the bribes this could be followed by blackmail threats of exposure to the German Commandant.

In March 1944 we received the shocking news that 51 prisoners from among the 80 who escaped through a tunnel from the North Compound of Stalag Luft III had been rounded up and shot on Hitler's express orders. This was effectively murder since these officers were protected by the Geneva Convention and it is the duty of all P.O.W.'s to try and escape and return home to fight on. After this disaster the senior British officer vetoed escape attempts on the grounds that it was a pointless waste of life. At least this had one small benefit. Our bunks had crosswise wooden slats to support the straw mattress we slept on, and there was a regular levy on these boards for lining a tunnel to prevent it caving in. After a time the bunks became decidedly uncomfortable with only a few boards to support the mattress.

On June 7th 1944 the German papers announced the invasion of Normandy. This worked wonders for our morale and we all visualised being 'home for Christmas' although an anxious few days followed until we heard that a firm bridgehead had been established. Soon after this on June 17th the newspapers announced the first use of their secret weapon, known as the V-1. This turned out to be an unmanned flying bomb with wings, a simple ramjet engine and a gyro stabilised steering system. Launched from the Pas de Calais area, it had enough range to reach London but could not be aimed accurately. When the engine ran out of fuel it fell to earth and exploded. We were naturally very worried about the damage this might do to London and the morale of Londoners, but newly captured prisoners arriving at our camp reported that the results were not devastating but obviously unpleasant for those in the area. Some of our newer fighters were fast enough to shoot them down or topple their gyros so that they fell in open country. The Germans too were developing faster fighters, and it was disturbing to see a twin jet-engined fighter over our camp one day (a Me 262). Less disturbing and very good for morale was to see a wing of American B-17 Flying Fortress bombers on their way to refuel in Rumania after bombing the Eastern German munitions factories normally out of range.

The telegram informing Oliver's parents of his capture

In the latter part of 1944 the advance of the Allied Armies in the West had met some stiff resistance from the Germans and slowed down considerably so that there was no prospect after all of being home for Christmas. The Red Army, however, after the hard fought victory at Stalingrad, was steadily advancing from the East. On a road which passed our camp we could see streams of refugees heading west with their possessions in hand carts, determined to keep out of Russian hands. We began to wonder what would happen next.

In late January 1945 we were warned to be ready to leave the camp at very short notice. We had enough time to make up some hard-tack rations from Red Cross food parcels, and to knock up some sledges out of old crates and hut

Gerrard 9234
HOLBORN
TELEPHONE: Extn. 311

AIR MINISTRY,
LONDON, W.C.2
W. 1.

Any communications on the subject of this letter should be addressed to :—

THE
UNDER SECRETARY
OF STATE.

and the following number quoted :—

P. 4 08157/43/1 P4 Gas B3

Feb: 24ᵗʰ 1942

Sir,
Madam,

I am directed to confirm a telegram from this department, in which you were notified that information has now been received through the International Red Cross Committee stating that your *son Flying Officer Oliver John Wells* Royal Air Force is a prisoner of war at a camp known as *Stalag Luft 4* in Germany. Your *son* will now be able to communicate direct to you.

A pamphlet regarding communication with prisoner of war is enclosed for your guidance.

(Sir,
I am, (Madam,
Your obedient Servant,

J. G. Shrewe .

for Director of Personal Services.

Sir Richard Wells D.L. M.P.

Kriegsgefangenenlager   Datum: 2-5-44

Dear Sir, I have today received from home the news of Oliver's safety. The crew & myself would like to join with you in voicing a prayer of extreme gratitude for what to us & much more so to you must be a miracle. Once again Sir, thank you for a marvellous skipper & thank God for his safety. Please pass to Oliver my best regards & sincere thanks for everything. Yours. F A G Clark

Postcard sent to Sir Richard Wells by one of Oliver's crew in captivity. It says a lot about the bond between bomber aircrew, irrespective of rank or social background, and the loyalty that Oliver generated amongst his crew.

---

furniture on which to tow our meagre kit and whatever food we could fit on. At 5 a.m. on the 29th of January we moved out of the camp in a column with armed guards on either side, towing our sledges through the snow. I was mighty glad of my R.A.F. greatcoat sent out from England. It was a strange sensation to be outside the wire in open countryside but there was no point in making a break for it as the situation was so chaotic and we were ordered to stay together for mutual safety. No rations were provided by the Germans but we had each been issued with a Red Cross food parcel on leaving the camp which enabled us to keep going. I believe we straggled along at about twenty kilometres a day, sleeping in locked farm barns at night in very primitive conditions with no opportunity to wash properly or shave but buoyed up by the expectation that it would soon be over with the Allies closing in from both east and west. The civilian Germans were not usually hostile, exchanging a bit of bread or hot water for cigarettes. At one point my little group (we tended to stay with our room-mates from the camp) managed to capture a hen which was boiled, feathers and all, in a metal water jug and shared out with great glee. After five days a sudden thaw made our sledges useless so we had to carry all we could and abandon the rest. On the seventh day we reached a place called Spemberg where we were put into empty cattle trucks – fifty men to a truck which meant we had to take it in turns to sit or lie down. The 60 mile journey to Luckenwalde too about 24 hours with frequent stops for air-raid alarms.

The new camp was just over 30 miles south of Berlin and was extremely squalid. There were groups of twelve three-tier bunks in each large room containing 200 men in all with no facilities for washing, heating, food or drink, and no Red Cross supplies. Life became very grim. The German rations amounted to one fifth of a loaf of black bread, half a litre of thin soup, a few potatoes and an ounce of margarine per day, about half the calorific value of a man's minimum daily requirement. We were all permanently hungry but able to survive by avoiding undue exertion. Worse was the absence of anything to do – no books and no news about what was happening outside, and no proper hygiene. I acquired a very bad attack of dysentery to add to the misery. No medical supplies were available either.

One redeeming feature was the nightly air raids on Berlin. We could hear the air raid warnings and see a satisfactory glow in the sky from the bombing. At this time the marvellous Mosquito aircraft was pasting Berlin from such a high altitude and speed that they were almost immune from attack. What a difference more of these aircraft would have made to the terrible casualties in Bomber Command if they had been available at an earlier stage in the war. With a crew of two they carried much the same bomb load as a B-17 Flying Fortress.

A delivery of American Red Cross parcels somehow began to filter through in about the middle of March and things looked up a lot. Also our secret radio bulletins started up again so we began to get some actual news instead of German propaganda about counter-attacks. On April 14th the Russians were getting close and the Germans tried to move us again. We were marched down to the cattle trucks at the local station from which we were supposed to be taken to Moosberg near Munich. This was worrying news as German transport was under heavy attack from the Allied air forces. Anxious by now to score some brownie points the Germans provided some yellow paint and allowed us to paint 'R.A.F. P.O.W.'S' on the roof of the trucks in huge letters. We were loaded into the trucks for the night but no engine could be found to move the train and we were marched back to the camp the following evening.

On April 21st the Russians were reported to be very close, the German guards all vanished and the senior British officer put into action a defence scheme, designed to keep the vital services of the camp going and ordered us to stay together for security. This seemed a very reasonable plan as there was absolute chaos in the countryside with armed S.S. units only too ready to fire on anything suspicious. When the Russian tanks arrived there was great excitement and some of the P.O.W's climbed up the camp fences to wave to them. As the Russian idea of liberating us was to mow down the fences with their tanks they had to jump off again in a hurry. The ordinary Russian soldiers of this unit were a fairly primitive lot, learning to ride bicycles which they had not seen before, and were a bit too keen to acquire our wristwatches.

As the Americans had reached the Elbe and had halted there we were confident of an early repatriation. After what seemed like interminable delays, a convoy of nineteen U.S. Army trucks arrived to take us west to the Elbe. Imagine our horror and frustration when the Red Army surrounded the trucks with guns, ordering us to get out again and even firing over our heads. The trucks returned empty to the Elbe and the Russians assured us that they would deliver us there shortly. The next few days involved the Russians making a list of all British prisoners, at which we individually decided to give false names as we had no wish by then to be on their records. I now believe that there was some high level negotiation going on involving the White Russian contingent who had been fighting with the Germans and were by then prisoners in Allied hands. There seems no other explanation for this extraordinary behaviour. In due course we were taken in Russian trucks to the Elbe and were then speedily repatriated, first to Brussels in Dakotas and then in Lancasters to England. Sitting beside the pilot as we crossed the coast of England I remember myself in tears of joy.

Here I must pay tribute to the magnificent work done by the International Red Cross. Without their efforts in very difficult circumstances I doubt that I would be writing this now and have always felt deeply grateful. It was good to be able to exchange letters with the brave and kind friends in Belgium whose identity I had kept secret from everyone until after the end of the war. I found that they were all intact, including Raymond Itterbeek, the young guide who was caught with us on the train. He had been condemned to death but was luckily held by the Wehrmacht who went by the book. As the Allies advanced he was moved from prison to prison and his papers failed to catch up with him.

The sentence was never carried out. In June 1947 I was able to visit Liege to thank my kind friends properly, and Fifi Fraipont came to England to stay at my home. Much later in 1994 I met Raymond Itterbeek in Brussels. He was by then Chairman of the Comet Line association of brave people who helped British and American airmen to escape. We had a long talk over an excellent lunch.

(After repatriation Oliver rejoined the RAF and was attached to the Central Bombing Establishment, flying types as varied as the DH Mosquito, Avro Anson and Lincoln. He also attempted a long distance record flight in a Lincoln 'Excalibur'. Sadly a failed engine over the Indian Ocean put paid to the attempt. Eventually he converted to Sunderland flying boats, joining 230 Squadron in time to take part in the Berlin Airlift).

Oliver's 'Kriegie' tag.

FLYING CARGO BOATS

AS MEMORIES OF THE GREAT Berlin airlift grow dim, it may be interesting to recall that a small detachment of Sunderland flying boats took part in Operation Plainfare, carrying their loads overland, like fish out of water, from Hamburg to Berlin.

It all happened very suddenly one damp July morning of 1948 in Ireland. We were based on a lake in Northern Ireland, carrying out routine anti-submarine training, when orders came through that we were to return to our base at Calshot at once, and prepare to leave for Germany. Leave for Hamburg we did too, at dawn the following morning, with as many spares as could be assembled in a few hours and a decidedly sketchy idea of the alighting area at Hamburg. This proved to be a fairly wide stretch of the Elbe about four miles down stream from the centre of Hamburg and our base was to be the old Blohm and Voss flying boat and seaplane factory, then occupied by the Royal Electrical and Mechanical Engineers, at Finkenwerde. The following day the operation started and the Sunderlands lumbered up the air corridor to Berlin, each loaded with 10,000lbs of food, to land on the Havel See, a large lake in the suburbs of Berlin almost alongside Gatow Airfield. This story must not be allowed to become a eulogy on flying boats, neither has the perennial land plane versus flying boat controversy any place in it, but here surely is a lesson in mobility. One day we were chasing submarines off Bloody Foreland, and within 48 hours the first Sunderland had landed a load of food at Berlin. No airfields, no spares other than those carried in the aircraft, not even any marine craft, and yet the loads were taken to Berlin almost without a hitch until the marine craft and spares caught up.

The Flying Task

The first few days of the operation were exciting. Nobody knew quite how the Russians would react to the thwarting of their blockade but Operation Plainfare was clearly distasteful to the Kremlin, and when Russian aircraft, probably merely intrigued by the sight of a flying boat in the corridor, came buzzing round it seemed probable that the cold war might turn unpleasantly hot. The effect of violent evasive action on 10,000lbs of 'meat and veg' might, we thought, be unhappy and more than one of us scanned the corridor very thoroughly for suitable stretches of water in case it became necessary to alight in a hurry.

As the days went by without incident, and we settled down into the routine of plodding up and down the corridor two or three times a day, this initial excitement gave way to more mundane but none the less keen competitions to do the quickest turnround, or head the list of sorties completed. The flight took about an hour each way, unloading on the Havel See between thirty minutes and an hour, and refuelling and reloading at Finkenwerde rather over an hour. The loading, unloading and refuelling required the presence of most of the aircraft's crew, so that three return trips to Berlin involved a long and arduous day and meals had to be eaten hastily on board the aircraft whenever time permitted. After refuelling at the end of the day in preparation for the morning, the ground crews would start their inspection, often working very late in their efforts to prepare the aircraft for an early start next day. Absence of any suitable lighting at either base made night flying impossible and so simplified the operation to a certain extent.

The base at Finkenwerde afforded quite a good alighting area, and provided that shipping and small boats on the Elbe could be cleared to one side, a long take-off run could be obtained up or down the river – although not necessarily into wind. With a full load on board some of the less lively aircraft required over 60 seconds at full power before they could be induced to leave the water in calm or cross-wind conditions, but the engines took the load manfully and rarely gave any trouble. The river traffic was considerable and many of the smaller boats, unable to understand the ways of flying boats, would chug cheerfully into the middle of the river in the path of an aircraft just about to touch down. A Royal Air Force seaplane tender, with the aid of high speed and some abusive language, unintelligible to the Germans but none the less effective, managed to keep most of the river traffic under control.

The flight to Berlin was simple enough, every village and road soon becoming a familiar landmark, and the navigators even stooped to flying the aircraft once they were satisfied that the pilots were capable of recognising the corridor. The countryside in the Russian zone looked strangely deserted and sinister from the air, although no doubt we looked on it with a rather jaundiced eye. A gentle landing on the Havel See was to be preferred, as the loaded aircraft were some 5,000lbs above the normal maximum landing weight, but since the lake was land-locked and always relatively calm this did not present any great difficulty. Occasionally there was a glassy calm, when it becomes impossible to distinguish the surface and so judge one's height, and the aircraft must be lowered onto the water in a landing attitude but with full flying speed. This naturally requires a considerably longer approach but fortunately the Havel See offered a long stretch of water in one direction that enabled this to be done quite safely. Normally the lake was quite clear, although at weekends a crop of small yachts sometimes complicated landing They were anxious enough to get out of the way, but the less skilled helmsmen sometimes lost control instead and could be seen gesticulating frantically at an approaching aircraft. The German river police, eager to exercise their authority in typical Teutonic style, rapidly towed such offenders to the shore, showering guttural abuse on them.

Since the lake was within a few hundred yards of Gatow airfield, where aircraft were landing at the rate of about one every two minutes, the sky in the

vicinity became somewhat exciting in poor visibility. Although we reported our movements to the approach control at Gatow, they found it impossible to co-ordinate the arrivals and departures on the lake with their own traffic stream and relied on us to keep out of the way. This we were only too willing to do and in bad weather the crews maintained a special look-out from the aircraft, one or two close shaves soon increasing their efficiency.

Base Facilities

Finkenwerde proved just adequate for the needs of the detachment, and the R.E.M.E, whom we considerably outnumbered, did all they could to provide suitable accommodation and messing. An operations room was hastily established in a tent by the pier and from this everything was directed. Aircrews were briefed, loads calculated, servicing cycles arranged, daily programmes drawn up and a hundred and one questions answered. In August the detachment was joined by two civil flying boats of the Hythe class, owned by the newly formed Aquila Airways. The crews lived and worked with us and quickly became very much a part of the detachment.

One of the main disadvantages of the base was the lack of a slipway, making it impossible to beach an aircraft except by deliberately grounding it in shallow water. Beaching may become imperative if the hull is damaged below the water line, and greatly facilitates changing an engine. There was an enormous crane, which could have picked a Sunderland out of the water 'by the scruff of its neck', but unfortunately the aircraft were not provided with suitable attachment points for this treatment. In the small harbour basin there was a hydraulic platform which slid under the water so that a flying boat fitted with beaching gear could be manoeuvred over it, and the platform then raised clear of the water level with the top of the bank. Unfortunately measurements proved that a Sunderland would only just fit over this platform and there was a decided risk that the lift would be set in motion only to reveal that one leg of the aircraft was not quite on the platform, with ugly consequences for the hull. Later on this lift was used successfully by attaching vertical poles to the corners of the platform so that they stuck out of the water, indicating the exact position of the platform eight feet below the surface in relation to the wheels and tail trolley fitted to the aircraft.

Until the arrival of the appropriate vessel, refuelling had to be carried out either by hand-pumping fuel from drums ferried out to the aircraft in army amphibians or by a floating pipeline brought out to a mooring buoy in the small basin. The German in charge of this pipeline was formerly a U-boat captain and he tactfully informed us that the only enemy he feared in the last war was Coastal Command. He soon found these remarks to be worth several cigarettes. In either case refuelling was complicated and slow, and the arrival of marine refuellers was most welcome.

Cigarette lighter presented to **Operation Plane Fare** aircrew by **The Berlin Chimney Sweeps' Association.**

The Load

The Army's Rear Air Supply and Forward Air Supply Organisations were

in full swing. To supply the freight at the right place and time, load the aircraft, unload them at their destination, and distribute the freight on arrival must have been no mean task, particularly as a great deal of German labour was used with its attendant language problem. The Army took all this in its stride and not only was the load always ready when wanted, but the efficiency with which the aircraft were loaded and unloaded and the good humoured co-operation which we always experienced from the Army personnel made our task infinitely easier.

The loading problem in itself was considerable. The freight had first to be loaded into boats small enough to be manoeuvred alongside the aircraft without damaging its hull and low enough to pass under the propellers. Fortunately, like all big river ports, Hamburg abounded in small diesel craft

coxed by boatmen who had been on the water all their lives, and several of these launches were hired and pressed into service at once. At first we watched these sixty foot launches, charging up to the hull as if they would smash it like an egg shell, with some trepidation, but it soon became apparent that the coxswains could manoeuvre their boats to the nearest inch and even in rough water the aircraft never suffered more than a few minor dents.

Next the Army, with the advice of the flight engineer, would distribute the load throughout the lower deck of the aircraft, mainly in the bomb-room, galley and wardroom, with a bit aft and in the forecastle for good measure. Finally the captain of the aircraft would look into the bomb-room and quail, shudder at the wardroom, glance at the galley and gasp and then climb the ladder to the flight deck muttering about engine temperatures on take-off. As soon as the aircraft was moored up on the Havel See at Berlin and the engines had stopped, a small motor boat would tow a lighter to either side of the fuselage, manned by German labourers who would clamber aboard to unload the freight.

Although the Sunderlands could only carry a modest 10,000lbs of freight, the inherent size of the fuselage made them ideal for comparatively light but bulky loads and quite a variety of goods came our way. There was, however, one minor disadvantage to the hull of the Sunderland. Under the floor of each compartment there are bilges, which are formed in a series of water-tight compartments and cluttered by a mass of longitudinal stringers to strengthen the hull. Inevitably some sacks, cartons and even tins burst asunder, and a proportion of their contents found its way into the bilges from which it could not be retrieved, even if there had been time, without a giant vacuum cleaner. Dried potato, canned meat, flour and various other basic foods of an equally un-appetizing nature sloshed about in the bilges, clogging the pumps, but otherwise harmless enough until we carried a load of yeast. Enough of this spilt into the bilges to start this un-savoury mixture 'working' and the resulting stench would have made Billingsgate fish market seem like a rose garden on a summer's evening. A large consignment of salt was allocated to us, on the grounds that Sunderlands were the only aircraft with anti-corrosive protection. Although effective enough against salt water, neat salt was too much for it and rust set in, making it necessary to flush out the fuselage with fresh water very thoroughly on overhauls.

Recreation

By taking a ferry over the Elbe and clambering into the back of a three-ton truck thoughtfully provided by the Army, we could reach the flesh-pots of Hamburg in about half an hour. The inhabitants of that city looked at our Royal Air Force uniforms rather sourly at first, as perhaps they might since about two thirds of their city was just rubble, but once they realised we were part of the airlift to Berlin their attitude became more friendly. A very fine officers' club, formerly the best hotel in Hamburg, afforded excellent food and drink, with soft lights and music, at a most reasonable cost. A country club in the suburbs, once the property of an industrial magnate, was also available. Styled with rather dubious taste, the outside walls were entirely covered with white tiles, like some gigantic public convenience, but the interior was most luxurious, and outside tennis courts and a swimming bath encouraged exercise. We had an American attached to us who was very keen to emphasise his Highland roots and frequently turned out in full kilt and Scots regalia to entertain the assembled company.

A form of exercise most congenial to the country lover was provided by the excellent duck shooting. At that time the Germans were forbidden to own any fire-arms, including shot guns, and large flights of duck would come into the small tributaries of the Elbe every evening. It was not uncommon to count fifty or sixty landing in some reeds only forty minutes' walk from Finkenwerde. Our marksmanship did not enable us to dine on roast duck very frequently, but the flights provided a very beautiful spectacle in the evening twilight.

Summary of Effort

In spite of the intensity of the flying there were no serious accidents during the detachment. The mooring area at Finkenwerde, which was in the form of a bay to one side of the main river, was rather shallow in places and, probably thanks to the bombing, somewhat encumbered with

Sunderland Mk V RN270 4X-0 moored on the Thames (©Aeroplane Magazine)

Oliver's fourth logbook. 3115 hours, 40 aircraft types and over fifty years of flying.

wrecks. This resulted in one or two instances of damaged hulls but in each case temporary repairs were made quickly enough to avoid the loss of an aircraft.

The flying boat detachment spent just over five months on the airlift and in that time flew over two thousand sorties to Berlin, covering nearly half a million miles and carrying about five and a half thousand tons of freight. The number of aircraft based at Finkenwerde fluctuated between five and eight, since they had to be taken back to England for all overhauls, and an average of four aircraft were available daily. In December 1948 the risk of ice ion the Elbe became acute and this, combined with the fact that Coastal Command were naturally anxious that the squadrons should resume their proper role, led to the withdrawal of the detachment.

Throughout this time the ground crews, living in conditions far from ideal and working hours that would have given any trades union official a heart attack, maintained a remarkable rate of serviceability and contributed a great deal towards the success of the operation. The aircraft themselves stood up to the unaccustomed role in a way which seemed to support the enthusiasm of their crews and all those on the detachment were proud to have contributed towards a very significant political victory.

Oliver Wells resigned his commission in the 1950's to take over running the family brewing business in Bedford, expansion and relocation of which he oversaw with great skill and distinction. He continued his flying career as a Trustee of the Shuttleworth Trust, flying many of the Collection aircraft until making his last sortie at the age of 72.

He still maintained a strong interest in aviation matters, being a regular subscriber to 'Aeroplane' magazine and keeping a Tiger Moth placard 'Aerobatics Are Permitted' in every car that he drove.

Oliver Wells sadly passed away on 4th June 2012 at the age of 90. He will always be one of that remarkable generation of gifted, yet modest flying heroes.

Excalibur - the Avro Lincoln in which Oliver attempted an endurance record from London to Australia.

Oliver's last flight at Old Warden, 3115 hours and 40 aircraft types on. His twin sister Sarah is in the front cockpit.

Models of two of the aircraft flown by Oliver Wells

Avro Lancaster B.III MG-N

Sunderland Mk V 4X-0

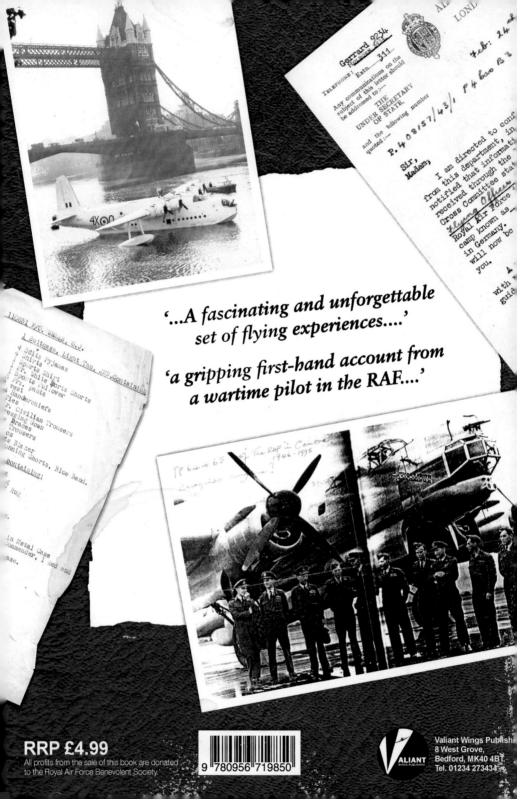

'...A fascinating and unforgettable set of flying experiences....'

'a gripping first-hand account from a wartime pilot in the RAF....'

RRP £4.99
All profits from the sale of this book are donated to the Royal Air Force Benevolent Society.

9 780956 719850

Valiant Wings Publishi
8 West Grove,
Bedford, MK40 4BT.
Tel. 01234 273434